"100% POSITIVE SPELLS AND INCANTATIONS FOR ALADDIN'S MAGICK LAMP"

By Maria D'Andrea MsD., D.D., DRH.

"100% POSITIVE SPELLS AND INCANTATIONS FOR ALADDIN'S MAGICK LAMP"

By Maria D'Andrea MsD, D.D., DRH

Copyright 2017 byMaria D'Andrea

Published in the United States of America By
Global Communications/Conspiracy Journal
Box 753 · New Brunswick, NJ 08903

Staff Members
Timothy G. Beckley, Publisher
Carol Ann Rodriguez, Assistant to the Publisher
Sean Casteel, General Associate Editor
Tim R. Swartz, Graphics and Editorial Consultant
William Kern, Editorial and Art Consultant

Sign Up On The Web For Our Free Weekly Newsletter
and Mail Order Version of Conspiracy Journal
and Bizarre Bazaar
www.Conspiracy Journal.com

Order Hot Line: 1-732-602-3407
PayPal: MrUFO8@hotmail.com

CONTENTS

YES YOU CAN SERIES

"100% POSITIVE SPELLS AND INCANTATIONS
FOR ALADDIN'S MAGICK LAMP"

By Maria D'Andrea MsD, D.D., DRH

DEDICATION

To Both My Supernatural Sons:

Both Rob D'Andrea and Rick Holecek have abilities that are beyond the five senses we normally utilize.

They are visionaries in their own right, as well as being inventive, compassionate, psychic and intellectual.

They can balance between this mundane world and other realms with ease.

Both are always supportive in all my endeavors and I feel blessed that they are my sons.

FOREWORD
By Robert D'Andrea

Maria D'Andrea decided to write this new book, *"100% Positive Spells And Incantations For Aladdin's Magickal Lamp"* to teach us about the Jinni. Some of you may have heard about this spiritual phenomenon, but whether you have or not, this book is guaranteed to pique everyone's interest. I was very excited when I found out what this book was going to be about. For a long time the Jinni has been an interesting and seductive topic to me. This is why I have been so anxious for *"100% Positive Spells And Incantations For Aladdin's Magickal Lamp"* to be published and I am sure that all of you who read this will feel the same.

"100 % Positive Spells And Incantations For Aladdin's Magickal Lamp" teaches us all about the nature spirit Jinni and how to call these powerful spirits in to use for our own advantage. Most importantly, we are taught how to do this in a positive and safe way. This is crucial because the Jinni can be very dangerous if not worked with correctly. Being that this is such an extremely ancient spirit, we will learn how to differentiate in order to deal with only positive Jinni. The Jinni is similar to the fictional character from fairy tales, "The Genie in the Lamp". Simply put, the Jinni

can grant any wish. People have free will and can make their own choices, but why not use every advantage at our disposal in a safe way?

After reading *"100% **Positive Spells And Incantations For Aladdin's Magickal Lamp"**,* we will know how to summon the Jinni to work on what we want to create for a better life. We will learn this from an extremely gifted and talented teacher who only deals with the positive and has been doing this for over 50 years. Maria D'Andrea is a very well-known and respected author in this field. She only teaches us what she has spent years learning, researching and perfecting on her own. Once again Maria D'Andrea has given us another fantastic and informative book that will help us better our lives and I'm confident that you will all feel the same.

USE THIS "ALADDIN'S" LAMP IMAGE
TO OBTAIN YOUR MOST SECRET DESIRES

While we highly recommend using our Magick Aladdin's Incantations Lamp to cast your spells or when performing rituals, it is nonetheless possible to use the above photographic image of a Genie's Lamp. Simply cut out the page or photo copy it. When performing a spell or ritual either gaze upon the lamp intensely or place your right hand over the photo while perform the specific spells.

The actual replica of the Magick Lamp (varies from that shown in photo) may be obtained by sending $27.50 + $5 s/h to Timothy G Beckley, Box 753, New Brunswick, NJ 08903

Conspiracy Journal
P R O D U C T I O N S

WE LIVE IN MAGICK

I was born in Hungary and I have lived and worked in the magickal kingdoms throughout my life. Even when I was a child, I would "know" or "hear" various spirits and beings speak to me. I would "feel" the wind shift, "see" or "feel" other elements and knew what it meant as a sign specifically for me.

I have always been tuned in, so to speak, to the vibrational frequencies of other realms.

It is just as though you are changing the stations on your radio until you get the one you are looking for.

We can "call in" the King of Salamanders (fire element), as an example, just as much as any other beings, including the Powerful Jinni.

These beings I have found want to help us, but we have to have the knowledge on how to deal with them so we never get hurt or give up control.

I'm always saying that knowledge is power for a reason. After all, if you don't know how to drive a car, are you going to jump in and not be aware of where the brakes are? Of course not.

I've worked with the Jinni for many years now, and I can tell you, that if done with focus, positive intent, will power to stick to it and conviction in the outcome, you can improve your life with their help in any area you wish.

Many of the formulae are my original ones, through my family and of course the ancient spells.

They utilize the word "wish" many times because what you wish for, even though not intellectually considered doable, can happen with the proper knowledge in the magickal realms.

We are non-limited spiritual beings in a physical body.

1

OUR MAGICKAL WORLD

Magick, as I always say to my students, is the oldest science. As an example: chemistry comes out of alchemy, physics comes from metaphysics also known as magick, occult (which just means ancient wisdom, hidden knowledge), the ancient arts. Magick is considered a science and an art. It is not religion.

Focus on your **own** belief system. You are the Divine Power. Remember, you have complete control.

Real magick has been passed down through the ages by word of mouth, by mystery schools like mine, Masters to Initiates (students), by families down to their descendants by word and what we call Book of Shadows (written formulae and information records not meant to go out of the family).

We have many secret Truths that are still to this day, taught only underground.

Mainly because spiritual, occult, magickal Laws and energies are neutral. We, as practitioners are positive or negative in how we work with these Laws. We are truly one or the other. It is like rain. Either it is raining or it's not. There isn't any in between.

However, there is a misconception that there is white and black magick. We do not adhere to that outlook. There is only energy and Universal Laws. We understand these Laws so we can create better lives and situations in a positive way that harms none. Think of it as rain again. If it is raining on a farm that has a draught problem, then the rain is considered positive. If it is raining and your next door neighbor is building an Ark, then not so much... Still it's just rain.

People in the magickal fields work on elevating themselves to a higher spiritual level of evolvement and do work on their own abilities.

We are creators of our own realities and co-creators with the Infinite Divine Power of the Universe. We understand the Laws of Nature and work **with** these Laws to create a better life for ourselves, those around us, our communities and our world.

We deal in cause and effect. If a formula worked centuries ago and gets passed down exactly as it is, it will have the exact same results every single time. If you deviate from the formulae, well... you never know what will happen, but it definitely will not give you the same results.

We also utilize tools when it is appropriate for the spell, formulae or ritual. These tools are charged over time. One of the reasons for this is so when you do use the same tool repeatedly, you need less of your own energy.

Some of us (who are like me-shaman, occultist, psychic, among my other abilities), also have our own formulae. We can create these because of our knowledge of the Universal Laws that we work with daily. If you don't understand what you are doing, you can get hurt and so need to be very careful.

This is why I **always** recommend before you delve into our mantic arts, you learn to do Psychic Self-Defense. You need to make sure you are always safe and protected in both realities of man and spirit.

Some magick in this day and age is diluted and incomplete and so, as expected, doesn't work. When you are protected, if things go wrong, you will still be safe.

You need to be prepared to penetrate into the magickal mysteries with respect, clarity, protection, a knowing of spiritual Truth, knowledge, positive intent, trust, will power and control over yourself and any situation around you.

AVOID THESE: Make sure you are dealing ONLY with positive Jinni. They can be dangerous if you "call in" the negative ones. Do not take them lightly.

You may think you can have control, but you cannot always with the negative ones always trying to take over control.

All of my books are always positive. We only do positive work and stay always on the Positive Path of Light, because Karma really does exist. In all spiritual systems of belief you will find this Law to ring true. What you do – good, bad or indifferent - will came back to you.

In ancient times, as well as now, formulae and heavier rituals are passed down through word of mouth. This is to ensure that you don't get hurt or worse.

WARNING: Take this work seriously with positive intent. This work is not a game.

We are dealing with the mysteries of life in our realm and other realms. We do not open a doorway without serious thought and intent.

Utilize my *"Prayer of Power"* for protection to keep you safe, or one of your own. This is your shield. This is your armor.

Prayer for Power

I am one with God
and let the power of God
flow in me,
through me,
and around me,
for God is All.
I trust the Divine Power
and all is perfect,
knowing I am always protected
and guided Divinely.
Whatever I choose
to manifest in my life
comes easily to me,
joyfully and with perfect
harmony.
I walk the path of White Light
in Truth, Peace,
Love,
Harmony and Health.
Thank you, Father, for I am
You are,
We are ONE.

Amen

by Rev. Maria D'Andrea

OTHER REALMS

The Djinn is also known as Jinn and Genie. These are a very powerful ancient race that we can work with from another realm. They have been with us in all cultures, even though when we think of these beings, we connect them to Aladdin and the Lamp.

The lamp is an old symbol of enlightenment and all that Light represents.

This is mainly due to the fact that they can be "called in" or called upon for any intent you can conceive. I look at it as - If you can think it, they can bring it.

The etheric realms can be traveled by the Jinni and by us. To work with the Jinn, it is better to have them come to you.

I've been to the other side so often; I can be a tour guide. They really need better road signs.

Some beings have a sense of humor, some do not. I've been to other realms and there isn't a way to describe how funny some are or how hilarious they look. Sometimes I think the cosmos just has a weird sense of humor and is playing with us.

On the other hand, some are dangerous and some are serious. The Jinni take things very seriously. We always approach them with respect still knowing that we are the ones in charge.

We need to understand who they are to be able to work with them. **I only have positive ones in my book**.

They are supernatural beings of power. They are connected mainly to stories about them in Arabian and Islamic theology. However, they are also connected to Asia, Egypt, North Africa, Korea, among others. They are known to reside all over the world. They can also be found living underground, in the deserts, hot burning sand, dust storms, woods, trees, seashores and wild places, among other areas.

Jinni are said to have been here about 2,000 years before Adam was created.

They are considered magickal beings, elementals and nature spirits.

They are said to be formed by tremendous heat, sometimes looking like smoke and are in both the non-visible and physical states. That is why so many people over the centuries have seen and interacted with them. Gigantic beings that can change their shapes at will to communicate in numerous ways and numerous forms with humans and they usually attach themselves to some form of light. (Hence, Aladdin's Lamp.) They can also take physical human or animal form and are able to work great illusions and have the ability to alter reality.

They communicate with not only us, but the animal kingdom as well. When flying quickly, they at times imitate the sounds of animals and humans.

Some Jinni can be vulnerable to such things as iron or copper.

*** Their desire is to work for human kind. ***

There are those who choose to work for mankind's benefit and those who harm. Your intent is of utmost importance.

You have to be aware to evoke only the positive ones because the negative ones are sly, devious, dangerous, aggressive, violent, greedy and obviously you cannot trust their word. Which is why I am always reminding you to "shield up" (use psychic self-defense in some form for protection).

Make sure your intent is pure and you stay spiritual and positive for this to work for you.

We thank them when we are done. In many of the spirit realms, thanking a spirit or Jinn is really a form of payment. Obviously they don't need money. However, when you thank them, you are sending love energy. Love is the most powerful force of energy. So sending love is sending a payment of love energy.

YOUR MAGICKAL TOOLS

The Jinni are powerful extraordinary beings. Decide what you "wish" to be your outcome and how you will approach gaining it before you call a Jinn. You have to be prepared and be able to focus.

Occultists have worked with these nature spirits for centuries. Few instruct the public on how to command them. Most people don't know too much about the Jinn and so don't have much interest. Mainly it is still an underground teaching, as in the old days. Occultists have been around for centuries and still are to this day. It is kept primarily underground because it can be dangerous, as I stated previously, to the initiate.

There is much preparation to being able to work with the Jinn forces safely and to be able to achieve your goals.

The preparation is not only a physical level, but also on a spiritual one.

Even though there are several paths to invoking a Jinni, we will work more directly to make it easier in the beginning. As you become more in control and more accomplished you can add on more rituals and spiritual tools.

Some tools for summoning include:

YOU !!! – You are all you need. You are the key. Everything extra is to aid you in your endeavors. Think of it as heightening your energy with a battery charger. A magician can do everything by his or her own powers, which has been gained through spiritual development.

*** Ceremonial magick can be added on and can be helpful. The advantage is that through the utilization of consistently using the same tools, the energy will be heightened in them and stored. The more you use them for the same purpose, the stronger the energy gets as it gets charged and attaches to the tool so that you can gain the same results with less of your own energy. ***

PREPARATION – Make sure everything is set before you begin. You can't stop in the middle of "calling in" to check on anything. You need control.

MEDITATION – Meditation is the link between man and the spirit realm. When you meditate prior to occult work, you are tuning into a different brainwave for a direct link to your Source and all realms.

When you speak normally to others your brainwave has scientifically been tested to be on a particular brain frequency. When we tune in on a magickal, psychic level, it shifts to a different frequency.

I love when the scientific community finds results to back us up. We have been doing occult and psychic work for centuries. It's about time they catch up a little. Some things just strike me as funny...

BRAINWAVES

Gamma = your fight or flight reaction

Beta = your everyday speaking to others

Alpha = your psychic, intuitive frequency

Theta = your deeper level of alpha

Delta = your deepest level. Such as a yogi slowing down his or her heartbeat, comma, and so on.

LOCATION – Some Jinni (or you) relate better to certain places, such as: seaside, mountains, valley and so forth.

MAGICK CIRCLE – One of the most important tools in ceremonial magick. It is always said that the occultist, magician stands in the center. One reason is for protection (I included my Protection Prayer earlier).

The circle represents man. The macrocosm and microcosm. The circle as the macrocosm represents infinity, the beginning and the end, endless. The circle is the Divinity in all.

The microcosm being the magician. When you stand in the center, it automatically connects you to the Divinity. One of my books - YES YOU CAN SERIES-on" EVOCATION" gives more exact directions.

Remember, YOU are the energy and MAGICK.

You can draw the magick circle with white chalk on the ground. Going toward the right until you connect back to where you started. If you break the line, simply restart. The line cannot be broken for your safety.

TRIANGLE – Symbol of manifestation. Manifesting spirit into the triangle. Connects to the mystical number 3= creating and creation.

You draw the triangle on the ground with white chalk first, outside of the circle. The spirit will manifest inside the triangle and will stay there until you banish it to go back to wherever it came from.

Start at the left bottom corner, up to the tip and back down to the right bottom of the triangle and lastly draw the line to the left connecting it to where you started. If you break the line, start again. If broken, it will not hold the spirit or Jinni.

To open the triangle after the spirit has been sent back, rub out the lines in reverse.

MAGICK LAMP – Symbolizes enlightenment, inner light, experience and understanding. When you light the lamp, you are lighting your inner light. (***Negative and low entities are afraid of the light. ***)

WAND, ROD, STAFF - Represents will. Symbolizes the magicians' power.

NUMEROUS TOOLS – Of course, there are many more tools and aids to utilize. We don't have to work with any or all by choice. As we go, I will tell you if any are needed for any particular Jinn. And so we now move on.

PROCEDURE

This is to give you an idea of the steps so it is not repeated at each formulae in this book.

Of course, there are more, but we are only working with the easier, less complicated spells to get you started.

These are proven, powerful formulae, as long as you stay positive, focused, in control, committed and expectant.

This will guide you to reach that pinnacle of success you are working toward achieving.

BASIC STEPS

It is recommended in rituals to cleanse your body first. At least, wash your hands. Focus on all negative psychic and physical influences running away from you with the water. At the same time, you are in essence doing the summoning with a clean body, clean soul and clean mind. This will put you more in tune with the Higher intelligences. It is not put as part of each ritual, but I suggest using this time to "attune yourself with the other realms."

1 - Clear purpose of the operation.

2 - The being and its abilities that you will evoke.

3 - The location you have chosen for working magick.

4 - Selecting and preparing any magickal tools needed for this operation.

*** When using a lamp or anything you have to light, remember never to put it out with your breath. This will not hurt the ritual, but will cancel it out. ***

5 - Putting up your psychic self-defense.

6 - Gaining your focus by meditation, slow breathing (3

deep, slow breaths or more) or any other technique preferred.

7 -   The drawing of the triangle.

*** You can use white chalk, or a staff or sword and draw in the ground ***

8 -The drawing of the magickal circle. Your attitude is connecting yourself with Divine Power as you do so. <u>You</u> are in charge of the magickal kingdoms. Your attention is on eliminating time and space within the circle. There are No limits.

9 - Placing your magickal tools, when needed, wherever they go.   (Sigil, incense, among other tools.)

10 - The magickal operation itself.

11 - Controlling the spirit, such as the particular Jinn you are commanding. Ordering the spirit to give you answers or to do a job.

*** <u>Note:</u> Know what the abilities are of that particular entity. You cannot command a spirit to help you with love, if the spirits ability lies with finance. It has a specific job. Call it in only for that situation. The Jinn wants to help, but can only do whatever its job ability is. ***

12 - Thanking or doing a prayer of thanks and dismissing the spirit.

*** In each ritual, you may say thank you or do a Prayer of Thanks that you created. Remember, it is a form of payment much as sending love angry. ***

13 - Opening the circle and triangle.

14 - Putting your tools where they are private.

15 - If writing in a Book of Shadows, this is the preferred time to do so.

*** A Shadow Book, is also called by other names, such as a Formulae Book. It is where you write your procedures, your feelings, how it went, what did or did not work. Any information to help you redo the operation, do it better or to avoid it. It is very personal and gets passed down through generations or sometimes used to teach Master to Initiate. It is meant as a memory aid. ***

***Remember, that even though you are the one in control at all times, you are dealing with high powerful beings. Do not misunderstand that because they will perform positive feats for you, that they are submissive. Stay serious throughout the rituals and remain in focused control. ***

MASTER YOUR FUTURE

We have a "knowing", faith. But as they say, "Faith without action is dead". We truly need both.

It is now time to take action. Dare to be in control of your destiny. Pick your Path. Let's go for it and make it happen.

You will get results by being positive and optimistic.

We have free will in the physical body, spirit does not. We have the wheel to control our direction and head toward new destinations

You are self-aware and can make positive choices in your life. Ignore others who are negative when they say: "you can't___". Of course you can. Nobody can block or stop you from your abundance and Divine right. They are not on your Path and are not ready to understand. That's alright; they are where they are meant to be at this point in their lives. You are way past it. There isn't any reason to explain anything that they probably won't understand. Just go about your business creating a better life.

*** Be sure to follow these steps: ***

1 - Decide what your intent, your goal, your wish is to be.

2 - "Know" that you are manifesting a positive outcome and that it's coming in. As you summon and command, it is already on its way to you.

3 - Focus your intent on creating with precision.

4 - *** Put up your PROTECTION. ***

5 – Never give up your power.

6 - Take the steps in the formulae for summoning and commanding the Jinn. Have no qualms.

7 - Thank the Jinn and send it forth to do your bidding.

You can add: go in peace and cause no harm to me or my loved ones.

8 – Look for it and expect it to manifest.

9 - Know that you are victorious.

MAGICKAL LAMP SPELL CASTING

SPELL INTENT: aids in gaining protection, strength and aids in all love matters. This spell also helps you to become rich by showing you what direction to go in.

This spell is to be cast on the new moon between the hours of 11:30 pm and 12:30 am.

Tools:

A lamp- can look like Aladdin's for great focus or any lamp. If you already used the lamp prior, place it in direct sunlight (such as on window sill or dresser that gets sunlight) for 3 days to cleanse energy that it's holding, to make a place for new focused intent .

White Chalk – any size. Unused.

Sigil for Lurchi: you can make a photocopy or redraw it.

Wear something white.

1 - Set the room up that you will do the summoning in. Make sure there will be no interruptions. Shut phones and other devices off.

2 - Meditate or just relax first.

3 - Wear something white.

4 - Do Protection.

5 - Place the Sigil and lamp in a spot where they will be within the circle when you draw it.

6 -Draw a circle, going toward the right, with you in the circle, until you connect it to where you started. If you break the circle in drawing it, start over again.

7 -Stand in the center of the circle.

8 -Place the Sigil (symbol representing this Jinn) on the floor in front of you.

9 -Hold the lamp, representing enlightenment in either hand. You can just hold it, or rub it for focus.

10 - In a commanding voice, <u>evoke Lurchi</u> to come to you. Say 3 times while gazing at the Sigil lying on the floor:

Lurchi of the powerful Jinn, I command you to come to me.

After the 3rd time, add your intention for calling him in. Remember to only invoke him for the purposes he is connected to.

11 - Allow a few minutes to feel the energy of the circle. You may feel a presence in the room. If you do, remember that YOU are in control. There is no fear here. You are protected within the circle. The Djinn will be on the outside and cannot come in.

12 - If you feel so, say your intent again.

13 - Now add - Thank you and go forth to do my bidding and do no harm to me or my loved ones. Go until I summon you again and you will come no matter where you are.

14 - At this point, put the lamp down; smudge the circle enough to give it a break in the line or all the line toward the left before you step outside it.

15 - Put the Sigil somewhere that others will not touch it until you summon Lurchi again.

QUESTING FOR ANSWERS

You are getting information in your dream state.

Sometimes, you may need a question answered. This question can be about anything. There aren't any limitations with the Jinni.

You can ask for the Jinns name, purpose or any other matter that comes to mind about any other subject.

Before sleep, when you are in bed, do Protection around you and the bed.

Decide on your question. Then with focus and command, do your summoning.

<u>Say with force:</u> I conjure the Highest power of Jinn for accurate answers to come to me now in a peaceful manner, doing no harm. Give me the answer to (<u>fill in with your question briefly and concisely)</u> in my dream state so it is understandable to me. Thank you and go forth when done.

You will get an answer within 3 nights. You may see the Jinn in your dream with the answer or simply get an answer. Sometimes, it triggers intuition also called your gut feelings, so pay attention to any urge or idea you may have all of a sudden.

CONJURING FOR BUSINESS / JOB

You are conjuring the Jinn called Pafessa.

Although you can conjure this Jinn at any time, the most powerful time is during the astrological time of Taurus.

Pafessa is excellent for any profession connected to work and lends advice and inspiration on how to improve in those areas.

Such as getting co-workers, bosses or employees to help you to do better. You never know how it will come in, but it will come.

Do your Protection first, as always.

Relax. You can take 3 slow deep breaths to do so.

Draw a circle with white chalk going toward the right with you and the Sigil for Pafessa within it.

Stand in the middle.

In a clear, commanding voice, 3 times say:

I call on Pafessa to come to me in peace and harmony, harming none. After the 3rd time, in a clear, concise way, state what you wish to be done.

Then add- Come to me quickly from wherever you are from now on when I call. Thank you Pafessa and go forth to do my bidding. Go.

OPEN DOORS INCANTATION

This evocation is to open doors in your life for opportunities to come to you and to give you inner freedom to gain victory.

Do this spell after it gets dark at night and before daylight.

Do your Protection.

Hold in your hand something gold. Doesn't matter what the item is. The gold is your focus.

Put your focus on your chosen purpose of doors opening and gaining freedom.

With force and focus, chant the following:

I now evoke the Jinn of power,

Come to me in this late hour,

By fire and Rain,

By earth and air,

Open all doors,

At my command.

In peace you come,

In peace you will leave,

Now, bring me victory,

So shall it be.

Thank you and go forth until I call again.

THE JINNI OF LOVE

Love is the strongest force of universal energy. On the physical, mundane plane it gives us a connection to others, picks up our mood and health, among other aspects.

In the other Realms of spirits, we send love as a form of payment and to thank whatever spirits we work with.

The Jinni connected to the love sphere are of incredible beauty and you are WARNED not to be so enthralled that you keep calling them in constantly. This eventually will cause a pact to be formed which will at some point limit your abilities and tie you to this sphere.

Make sure you have the ability to resist through spiritual evolvement, so you can conjure different Jinni to create other goals.

Love energy can be romantic love, friendship, family, pets and any and all forms.

Make sure you know exactly what you wish to manifest into existence.

SPELL OF ISODEH

The Jinn called Isodeh, is connected to love magick.

Isodeh inspires love and its actualization. This Jinn brings love energy, not only uniting people, but also love energy with all beings in all the Realms.

Procedure:

Hold the Sigil for Isodeh in either hand. Draw this sigil in green.

Spend a few minutes looking at the Seal, with focus. You will have the urge to stop looking when it's time.

With purpose and in a commanding voice, say:

I conjure and command Isodeh to come to me now, in a positive and peaceful manner.

Come and carry out my wishes speedily and correctly with love.

I now have mastery over you. I direct you to (fill in what your intent is, in a clear manner).

Bring this to fruition in a way that's positive for all, harming none.

Thank you and go forth.

When you are finished, put the Sigil in a place where nobody will touch it until the next time you need it. Otherwise, you can burn it to ashes and throw it to the wind.

COSMIC LOVE

The Jinn named Odac is known for connecting to cosmic love and helping you to unite with the Divine Power for the purpose of achieving and perfecting yourself, with the utilization of rituals.

Your ability will also be enhanced in applying this energy in the mental, physical and astral planes.

To begin:

1 -As usual, go to a place where you will not be disturbed.

2 - Do your Protection.

3 - -Start with slow breathing. This is for accumulating power and relaxation. (This breathing can be used before all endeavors.) It is a form of energy charging. Do this until you have the urge to stop.

4 - Get some incense and a holder. It can be Frankincense, Musk, Orris, Roses or Patchouli. Take it into your circle.

5 - Draw your Sigil in gold, yellow or a bronze color. Or make a copy of the one in this book and color over it.

6 - Take your Sigil for Odac in either hand and take it into the circle.

7 - Draw your magick circle with white chalk around you, going toward the right until you connect the lines. Remember, if your line gets disconnected, redraw it. It cannot be broken to let in the Jinn.

8 - Place the incense with incense holder on the floor. Light your incense inside the magick circle, focusing on your positive intent. This not only sets the mood, it also attracts the spirits as a magnet.

9 - Place the Jinn Sigil for Odac next to the incense.

10 - Stand in the center of the circle.

11 - Look at the Sigil with your attention focused on it for a few seconds or however long you feel.

12 - Now, evoke in a loud voice, the Jinn with a command:

I now call forth Odac to do my bidding. Come to me now in a calm, friendly manner, harming none.

I command you thus:

Bring to me the ability to connect to cosmic love and to elevate myself to a Higher spiritual level. To gain access to the Divine with me, that I know is there. To move me forward to spiritual victory.

Do this easily, harmoniously and positively now.

Thank you Odac and go forth until I summon you again.

13 - Put out the incense. Pick up the Sigil.

14 - Going toward your left, open the circle by rubbing it.

15 - Throw what's left of the incense to the wind.

16 - Put the Sigil in a private place for future use.

YOUR WISHING LAMP

Make a copy of the Lamp in the front of this book.

Pick your intent in ANY AREA YOU SO WISH. Remember that there are no limitations in the other realms. The only limits you have are the ones you set on yourself.

Don't focus on how your wish will come in. Only on what the outcome is that you desire.

It doesn't matter what time of day or night you do this ritual, but try to do it around the same time each day. If you cannot, then at least do it each time during the day or night. This is not necessary, but adds to the energies to heighten them.

Hold the copy of the lamp in between both hands and focus on your intent. Make sure you are calm, in control and always positive. Focus so much that nothing else is noticed. Not your location, sounds, or anything else on the mundane, physical plane. Block out everything else except your purpose.

Rub the lamp 3 times while focusing. The lamp is there to remind you of the Light within, enlightenment and to Light your way to your wishes. It is a focal point to aid you in your concentration.

It has its own energy imprinted on it by centuries of people knowing what the lamp represents and utilizing it for that purpose.

When you are finished, place your lamp anywhere it will not be touched by others in the Eastern section of your home.

*** Take it out and redo this ritual every day for 50 days to create the changes you wished for. At the end of that time, take the lamp and burn it to ashes. Next, throw it outside to the wind. ***

GET WHAT YOU WANT SPELL

Who says you can't get what you want? Not me...

Have you ever noticed that some people genuinely wish you the best? Those are wonderful, positive people. Then there are those who want you to do well, but not better than them. Next are those who just don't want anyone to be happy at all.

Well, we don't let anyone slow us down or bock us from our goals. We learn not to tell others what we are working on ahead of time. We go our happy way and just manifest everything we wish for. We can always tell them afterward. But why? There's no need to do that.

We have free will to do as we wish. We work with the Laws of Nature in a positive way. We are the bold, discovering secrets that will unfold the natural ways of the universes to become co-creators of our lives.

You are at the beginning of your new life. So, let us move forward in making the right choices. Define yourself and your new goals.

Imagine living the life you wish for. The life you truly deserve. Yes, I said you deserve it. Even if you don't feel like that at this moment, Divine Power does and is right there for you. A little like having your own cheering section. Yay !

Now, down to creating and changing the game of life to be in your favor:

1 - Get a lamp or copy the picture of the lamp in the front of this book.

You have strong spiritual energy and you are going to utilize it now.

2 - Do your Protection.

3 - Do slow, deep breathing for at least 3 breaths. More is good, but less won't work.

4 - Pick your goal. Go ahead, pick one you really want.

5 - Now, that you have one in mind, pick up and hold the "lamp" in either palm.

6 - Look down on the lamp. Visualize a tornado in the center. Now, mentally focus on your intent for 60 seconds or so and then mentally sink it into the tornado.

7 - Next, visualize the tornado sinking into the lamp until it is all inside the lamp.

8 - Now, it's time in a calm, commanding voice to <u>call in the Jinn, say:</u>

I command and summon the Master JINN of the Highest Order for the purpose of <u>(say what your wish is)</u>. I command and order you to fulfill my wish speedily, easily and harming none.

Go now at my bidding to do your work. Go in peace until I summon you again.

Thank you and now go forth. Go!

9 - Take your lamp and place it in the back of your closet until it comes to fruition.

10 - Redo visualizing the tornado effect on and off.

KNOWLEDGE IS POWER

You can gain knowledge in any form such as with business, hobby, fun, how to make a better living (after all, we are spirit but in a physical body. You still need health, food, shelter, clothing, transportation, among other physical things), to name a few and your life will improve by leaps and bounds.

The more knowledge you have, the better your decisions will be and your life will take an upward path.

To gain this knowledge in any area, you will summon the Jinn known as Ambriel.

Purpose: He is considered the chief of the mind and all intellect. This includes the theoretical outlook of all science, perception, understanding and the arts.

We evoke Ambriel for all sciences, including the occult and mantic arts.

The Summoning:

Enter into your private location and make sure you will not be disturbed.

Place something with the color yellow into your area.

Enter into your slow breathing state for at least 3 breaths to connect you to your Inner Kingdom.

Focus on your Intent clearly.

Put up your protection.

Be ready to receive the knowledge. Be willing to receive it. Then you are open and able to receive it.

Command in faith the following:

I summon you, mighty Jinn, by your name AMBRIEL!

I call on you to elevate my knowledge, understanding and wisdom in all areas (or put a specific area, such as mechanics, school and so on) which you control. Bring your supernatural powers to my aid.

Unlock the secrets of the universe to rapidly accelerate my learning.

Give me supernatural access to expand my consciousness.

I command you to begin this very instant.

Thank you Ambriel and go forth and hurt none. Until I summon you again. Go.

You are now finished, walk away in faith.

ILLUMINATING THE ABYSS OF YOUR LIFE

There are times in our lives when we feel like we've dropped into a bottomless pit. We have all been there. But this is when we need to get ourselves up and on the move upward toward the spiritual Light that illuminates the darkness.

This Jinn originates from the Light Sphere and will bring you the Light that is needed in your life right now.

The Jinn is called the "Master of the Sun Sphere" and is the ruler over 45 Jinni. He is better known as Mettatron in the Quabbalistic system. Either name will suffice.

Mettatron is considered the mediator between man and the Creator (God). He brings enlightenment to those who are seekers. You will be able to rise above the mundane and deal with any issues that may arise in your life. Power will come to you with your connection directly to Mettatron and God.

With this combination in your corner, how can you fail?

Mettatron will lift you out of your abyss and bring you into the Light.

The Ritual

1 - When summoning Mettatron, have something golden yellow, small enough to carry with you later, to take into the circle with you as an energy point of focus to be charged automatically during the summoning.

2 - Do your Psychic Self-Defense so nothing else can come though the portal when you are doing the summoning.

3 - Focus on golden yellow light as you take a breath in and gray light as you breathe out negativity. Do this for a few minutes until you have the urge to stop.

4 - Surround yourself with the golden yellow light and have it permeate throughout your body. Let it stay there as you go to your next step.

5 - With white chalk, draw your triangle. Start, as usual, from the left bottom corner, to the top of the triangle and back to the right bottom. Next, go to the left connecting and closing it off. Make sure you don't break the line. This is where the Jinn will manifest.

6- Draw your circle with the white chalk around you and the golden yellow item you picked earlier, going from the right until it is connected to the start. Remember, if you break the line, simply redo it. It has to be completely closed. Stand in the center and place your golden yellow object near you. Get focused and expectant.

To evoke this powerful Jinn with control, command thus:

I, (say your name), place this evocation with you, Mettatron, the Master of the Sun Sphere, to come to me now in a peaceful, harmonious way, harming none.

Know that I require and command you to bear me up out of this abyss with your Illuminating Light to that pinnacle of success that I desire.

You shall begin this very instant to shape the future to bring me out of the darkness and into the Light.

By the power of these words and invocation, be ruled by me.

Go now and be ready to come when I call you.

Thank you Mettatron, now go in peace.

7 – Open the circle by rubbing part or all of it away going toward the left.

8 - Open the triangle the same way.

9 – Keep your charged item with you at all times.

HEALTH THE JINN WAY

All forms of healing work in the same manner. It doesn't matter if you go to the medical field, holistic, acupuncture, energy healing or any other healing treatment.

They all work by speeding up your natural healing energy.

If you truly wish to be healed, this will speed up the healing process. If you are not ready to be healed, the energy will simply go through you without harm.

An <u>example</u> of a case I worked on:

A lady kept getting extreme headaches, migraine headaches, every time she was invited to a party. The headaches were very real. She consciously wanted to go see her friends and hated to turn down the invitations. In fact, she would say to her husband that he should go. She meant it, but he didn't go, saying how it would look that he went and left his sick wife at home. She felt sad about it, but she was in real pain. I noticed it was only when there was an invitation to a party.

It turned out that when she was a child, her parents would take her to adult parties where she was ignored and told to be silent all the time. She always felt hurt and unimportant. This reaction was subconscious, but prevented her from going in case the same situation would arise. Of course it wouldn't, but again, it wasn't conscious.

Once she realized and was open to healing, knowing the situation wouldn't come up with her as an adult, her headaches were healed.

<u>Healing Ritual:</u>

Wear something green or pink.

33

Get a stone called Red Jasper. If it is not available, a piece of green stone like Jade or Aventurine will do. Wash it off for later use.

Shield up. (Protection)

Hold the stone in your dominant hand (the one you write with).

Do the summoning:

1 – Stand with the healing stone in your hand.

2 – Say in a clear, commanding voice:

I call forth the Master of the Highest Jinn Order for Healing. Come to me quickly, peacefully and with a positive healing attitude.

Through the power of this Jinn Master, I now command the atomic and molecular elements inherent within air, earth, water, fire and spirit with my one desire and clear intention, which is to be quickly healed. (At this point, you may specify a particular health issue or just leave it as all healing in general.)

I have the warrior energy of my ancestors and knowing that their blood flows through me, I now conjure the healing energies with the Master Healer of the Jinn.

Thank you and go forth until I call you again.

3 – Take the stone and put it into water. You can put it into a gallon container, as an example. Leave it in there for 48 hours.

This will charge the water with healing energy. After you take the stone out, you need to save it for the next container of water.

4 – Each time you drink, visualize the water as green healing energy, flowing throughout your body to speed up healing.

Drink at least 1 glass at night and 1 in the morning. The more you drink the better and quicker.

BE THE JINN YOU ALWAYS WANTED TO BE

Who says you have limits? Pick your goal. You are going to grant your own wish by focusing on intent, keeping it going by will power, "calling in" help and expecting it to come in, always in a positive way.

I think at this point we need to evoke the Jinn named Hagiel for friendship, love, luck and success.

That should cover a lot of ground, wouldn't you say? You know you want success or you wouldn't be adding on help, so let's get started on this adventure into making your life easier and better.

Summoning Formula:

1 – This ritual is best performed on a Friday or Sunday (the time doesn't matter).

2 – Find your location so it is private and nothing will disturb you.

3 – Have a lamp or some form of light ready to take into the circle with you. And take something to put the light out without using your breath.

4 – Make sure of your intent.

5 – Focus your intent by washing your hands and visualizing all negativity that blocks you or slows you down being swept, cleansed away with the water. Focus on your mind, body and spirit being cleansed.

6 – Take 3 slow deep breaths to get relaxed and calm.

7 – Draw the Triangle with white chalk, going left bottom to top point, to right bottom of triangle and toward the left to where you started the line. This is where the Jinn will manifest.

8 – Draw with white chalk the magickal circle around you while holding the lamp or some form of light. Drawing the circle toward the right.

9 – Once the circle is completed, stand in the center.

10 – Light the lamp or equivalent. This represents the light within and your connection to God. Everything we do comes through the Divine Power to keep everything safe and positive.

11 – Now, do the <u>summoning</u>-

I summon the Jinn known as Hagiel to come to me now in a peaceful and positive manner.

Hagiel! Hagiel! Hagiel!

I call on Hagiel, spirit and Jinn. Hagiel,I command you to shape the future so that you bring me success in all of my endeavors through the power of your abilities.

Thank you.

Go now, and come whenever I call on you. Go in peace and harm none.

Go!

12 – Know that Hagiel is working for you. Keep your eyes out for opportunities to emerge or luck to appear. Make sure you pay great attention to any gut feelings you may have and try to move on them.

If you call for help, you need to listen and pay attention to the insights leading you toward your goals.

After all, if you ask a friend for help or ask a question, you normally pay attention to the answer.

13 – Put out the light. Remember, not to blow it out with your breath, use something to cover it to snuff it out.

14 – Open your circle by rubbing out an opening to walk through or rubbing it out going toward the left until it's all open.

15 – Open the triangle the same way.

JOYFUL MODE OF LIVING

Sometimes we need to change bad living conditions into good ones. This also will enhance your life to be much happier. You want to bring in joy, harmony and balance.

What your living conditions are influences how you feel, how you interact with others and the joy, or lack thereof, in each day as you go forward in life. So let's make some changes and bring in some overdue fun.

This is your wake-up call to improve your situation right now.

The Jinn named Kofan is your connection to changing your condition.

Formula:

1 – Find a quiet, private location to do the summoning, where you will not be bothered by anything, such as the phone ringing, people or any other disturbances.

2 – Put up your psychic self-defense protection-shield up!

3 – Focus your intent by visualizing, with your eyes closed, a little above your physical eyes, about 3" in front of you and to the right about the situation you now have. Only for a second.

4 – Now, shift your eyes (still closed) to your left, focus on the outcome that you wish for. The outcome you are now in the process of manifesting into physical reality.

Do not hesitate to make it as clear and colorful as you can. Add in the details.

5 – Next, consciously become aware of what you would feel emotionally when this occurs. Allow yourself to feel happy, joyous, exuberant. After all, isn't that how you'd feel? Of course

it is.

6 – With sincerity and command, verbally, do the evoca-tion:

I now call on the Jinn Kofan, connected to the 21st degree of the astrological sign of Scorpio.

Kofan! Kofan! Kofan! Of the Jinni, come rapidy now to me in peace, in a comely form and harm none.

I command you to manifest all the positive changes I wish to make to my living condition in joy and happiness. To bring about these changes swiftly and all in my favor, in only a posi-tive manner.

Thank you.

Kofan, I know you're swift and true, go forth now until next I call on you and do my bidding.

7 –Be conscious of your situation being resolved and im-proved upon. Be ready, willing and looking forward to your breakthrough results. Pay attention to any intuitive gut feelings you may have and move on them.

You may have an urge, as an example, to go out of your way to be nice to a terrible landlord, to later find he or she was mean because of feeling all alone. Something as little as that may start the changes.

Know that the changes are on the way. Kofan never fails you.

THE PLEASURES OF LIFE

The Jinn to summon is named Nesi. Nesi is connected to the 5th degree of the astrological sign of Taurus.

This powerful Jinn makes life full of pleasure. (Such as increasing income, improving your position in life, gives advice through your intuitive senses, among other ways.)

<u>Summoning</u> the Jinn Nesi:

Do your psychic self-defense protection prayer.

Run your hands under water to realign your energy with your focus on positive only, in your body, spirit and mind. The water takes away all negativity around and within you. (After all, we are human, who never has a negative thought?)

Hold something in your hand that connects to the earth. Such as a stone, rock, dirt, sand, anything that is energy connected to the ground you stand on.

Visualize yourself standing on a mountain top. (If you can, it would be of benefit to physically stand in such a spot.)

Do the <u>following</u>:

I <u>(say your name),</u> command that you, a Master Jinn , Nesi, appear before me rapidly, in a comely manner, peacefully and harming none.

I command that you make my life more pleasurable and agreeable to me Start at this very instant to bring in the results that are positive for me. I call forth your powers to heighten, elevate and improve my life.

In the name of Divine Power, I command you.

In the name of the elemental and spirit kingdoms that are your realm and the unlimited universe, I command you.

In faith, I command you.

I (say your name), command you.

Go forth and create the future that is mine by Divine Right until I summon you again.

Thank you for your work on my behalf.

GO!

Take the earth related item in your hand and place it back onto the earth, the ground. If you are in a city and cannot do so, the street is the same. It is made up of the materials from the earth.

Take a deep breath and walk away. It is done.

ESCAPE YOUR PRISON OF DIFFICULTIES

It is time for you to summon the Jinn known as Schaluach.

This powerful Jinns job is to help with intuition the one who did the summoning. Schaluach helps in the most difficult situations, where there isn't any escape under normal, every-day circumstances.

This is the Jinn to summon when you've tried the normal, mundane, everyday methods and they haven't worked.

Draw the Seal of Schaluach in the color green. You can photocopy it and draw over it with green and your clearly focused intent.

The Evocation:

In the Power of the Divine, I place this invocation with thee, Schaluach, Jinn of intuitive guidance to change all unmanageable situations.

Know that I require and command thee to give me insight to escaping from (say the difficulty to change).

Thou hast dominion over these difficulties and thou shalt begin this very instant to shape the future such that my difficulties are no longer. In a way that harms none.

By the power of these words and invocation, be thou ruled by me.

Go until I summon thee and create my future.

Go forth!

Pay attention to your intuitive, gut feelings. You summoned the Jinn to heighten your ability and to move your mountains, so to speak. Take this seriously to gain your escape.

41

WEALTHY WAY

Wealth comes in many guises. It can come as opportunities through jobs, through a windfall, luck, intuition, or any other form of abundance flowing into your life.

We keep ourselves open to these flowing energies and move on them when they manifest for us.

When you are an open door, you never know what incredible life transforming situations will come up.

You are blessed and Divine Power, God will stand with you, when nobody else will. He gives you connections to different realms, such as to spirits, angels, elementals, Jinni to help move you up and open the doors to your abundance.

Set your mind on peace and prosperity.

Do your protection as always.

Your mindset: Prepare for the things you have asked for when there isn't a sign of it in sight. Know and trust that it is yours.

The conjuring:

I summon the Master of the Highest Order of Jinn in peace and harming none, to manifest wealth into my life, in a positive way.

I command the Master of the Highest Order of Jinn to smash and abolish in a positive way, by my spoken word, every untrue record in my subconscious mind that stops, blocks or slows me down from my rightful wealth. These thoughts shall return to the dust heap of nothingness for they came from my own imaginings.

Unlimited Jinn, open the way for my wealth to come to me

under Grace and in a perfect way rapidly.

I command you in the name of Divine Power.

Go forth and do my bidding.

Remember to say thanks and take a few deep, slow breaths and walk away, knowing it is done.

For the next 3 weeks, be aware of your thoughts concerning wealth. Your subconscious will try to fight the new positive way. Whenever you find a negative thought concerning wealth, mentally use the word "cancel", replace it with a positive wealthy thought and trust that the Jinn is working on it on your behalf right now.

OCCULT LAWS FOR A HEALTHY DIET

In the blink of an eye, you can master the correct diet for yourself.

The Jinn, named Camarion, will give you insight on which foods you should to eat.

The Law of Similarities or at times called Law of Analogies helps you to gain healthy habits to balance your energies. Healthy in your spirit or astral body, mental body, as well as, in your physical body.

You will automatically start to move in the direction of the weight you should be to have balance. It is good to also drop, or gain weight, depending on your goals.

When called upon, this Jinn will help you reach for the correct foods to have positive impact on improving your health when needed.

When you conjure Camarion, pay attention afterward to any urges or feeling you may have. If you ask, you need to listen and move on the insight given.

As an example: you have a shopping list to go to the supermarket. You have a plan on what you are having for dinner, snacks, and so on for the week. You get to the market and as you go to pick up an item on your list, it just doesn't feel right. You aren't sure why, but you question it now. You're thinking, but it's on the list for a recipe so I need it.

What you are feeling is the insight that a particular item isn't good for you at this is time. So, since you called for help with Camarion, PUT IT DOWN. You know you should, right?

Now, in the other direction, if you are passing an item and have an urge to pick it up, then do so, because at this time,

44

your physical, mental or astral body needs whatever is in that food.

At times it has to do, not only with the obvious ingredients, but also with the magnetic or electric charge it holds.

Sometimes, you may have noticed you are looking at a bin with apples and even though there are many that look good, certain ones just feel right for you.

Now, you have the guidance to pick exactly what will be the very best to improves your health, balance your energies, gain or drop weight and create harmony within you.

Procedure:

1 – Put up your shield of protection.

2 – Wear something with the color green.

3 – Hold the stone called red jasper or a green stone, such as jade in either hand while performing this ritual.

4 – Wash your hands and let the water run onto the stone, cleansing all negativity out of the stone and any of that negative energy around and in you. Do this until you feel an urge to stop.

5 – Find a secluded spot, preferably outside connecting to nature. Anywhere where you will not be disturbed is fine.

6 –Make sure you have your purpose set in your mind.

7 –Since you know you are on an upward move, have a happy feeling before you begin the conjuring.

8 –Take your 3 slow, deep breaths or do meditation to relax and tune into your alpha state of mind.

9 – So, in a loud and commanding voice, let's get to the conjuring:

I conjure and command thee, Jinn Camarion to come to me now. Come in a pleasing form and in peace and harmony, harming none.

Camarion, I conjure thee to come from your domain to me instantly now and every time I call.

I command thee to construct the electromagnetic fields and electrical fields to heighten and balance my health in my

45

body, mind and astral form. To bring insight to me at all times on what to choose to eat to achieve these intents.

Bring guidance in the form of instinct and intuition so that I may improve on all of these levels (and – say what issue if any, you have at this time to improve, such as dieting, a health issue, and so on).

I command thee to now charge the stone that I hold in my hand for the intent I have given to you.

I conjure thee thus: Obey and do my bidding and come rapidly whenever I call. Bring me to the height of my success NOW.

Thank you and go forth in peace to do this, my focused intent.

And as by my will, so it is.

When you are finished, take the stone of your choosing and carry it within 3' of your body at all times. It is a container of energy that was charged during the ritual and holds your intent and will aid in triggering your insight.

Whenever you need a conscious reminder or help to keep on track, simply touch the activated stone.

LAWS OF MIRACLES

The real miracles are not the ones you often think of when working with the Jinni. However, we connect with the Jinni, and other realms because we are all connected to Nature's Laws and so have the ability to work together, in various ways.

There aren't any supernatural occurrences, because everything in nature is possible by natural laws and by spiritual powers.

What causes the miracles is simply having the knowledge of the Laws of Nature and working with these Laws to create what our intent is focused on.

Remember, we are the oldest science. We work with cause and effect. With alchemy, physics, the physical and non-physical realms of existence.

We travel the visible and the non-visible energy streams of the unlimited cosmos.

We are the travelers of the realms and the adventurers of the unknown.

We are creators of our future when we have the knowledge to do so. We work with nature, knowing the outcome is definite as we create our intents.

We move forward in both worlds. We are connected to the Divine and walk the tightrope between the two realities of man and spirit. We are "consciously" choosing which reality to be in, at which time.

This is why we are known as psychics, occultists, magi, shaman, and masters of the unseen realms that are everywhere.

We are all constantly evolving.

This is how true miracles occur.

Now, to conjure a miracle:

1 – Wear something white.

2 – Wash your hands and focus your intent.

3 – Shield up! Do your protection prayer.

4 – With white chalk, draw a triangle on the ground. Or use a staff or sword to draw in the earth. Start drawing your triangle from the left bottom point, then to the tip at the top and back down to the bottom right, next go left until it connects to the starting line. This is to contain the elemental nature spirit, known as the Jinn.

5 – With white chalk, draw your magick circle. Start drawing toward the right, around you, until you completed the circle back to the beginning line.

6 – Stand in the center of the circle, as always.

7 – Begin the summoning:

I now summon and command the Jinn known as Ezhobar. To come to me peacefully and in harmony, harming none.

Ezhobar ! Ezhobar! Ezhobar!

I command you to reveal to me the secrets you hold of creating, of manifesting all my desires and wishes, easily and effortlessly.

Bring the miracle I seek to me through the positive Laws that you adhere to, for the purpose of (state what you are manifesting into your life).

Do this swiftly, and through your powers.

Teach me through inspiration and intuition how to bring about the knowledge of the moon spheres, which you are connected to for understanding symbols and heightening intuition.

I command you thus: go forth and do my bidding now and come to me each and every time I summon you, quickly and peacefully.

Thank you and go forth.

8 – At this time, spend a minute in thankful prayer or thought.

9 – Open the circle by smudging the chalk line, or the line in the earth, in reverse order, toward the left.

10 – Step out and open the triangle in reverse order.

11 – Walk away and don't look back.

KEYS TO THE JINNI

As someone connecting to the realm of the Jinni, you have to be very careful. I only put the positive Jinni in my book. However, remember there are the negative ones and the ones we look at as tricksters.

The main reason I keep saying that some form of protection is needed, is to keep you safe on all 3 levels. Your astral body, physical body and mental body.

Even though we are only dealing with the positive Jinni, you are still opening a doorway. And as with any open door, as the one you call comes through, another can sneak in and hitchhike through the opening.

The protection keeps negative at bay and they cannot harm you or even enter.

My "Prayer of Power", in the beginning of the book is for your protection. Say it with conviction and as a statement of fact.

If you have a different name for your Highest Power, instead of God, feel free to substitute the name you normally use. It has to match your vibrational energies. We look at it as there is One Source, we don't care what label you use to connect with that Source.

Be aware at all times that you are the one in control, because you are in the physical body with free will. You are also the practitioner who commanded the Jinni to come to you. You always have to remember to send it forth in some form. How you say it doesn't matter. It can be –thou- or a slang word. The outcome is the same. You are not insulting them.

IF you called, the Jinni comes. You have to send them back

50

or they cannot leave. It's *** <u>imperative</u> *** that you release them to go and do what you commanded of them.

They want to help mankind. It is up to you to have the knowledge to know which Jinn is connected to which ability to serve you. As I've said previously, you cannot ask a painter to help you as a financial advisor. It's not the right job and so that particular Jinn cannot do it.

Your intent, your purpose, has to be very clear and concise before you begin. If you were in the military giving an order, you wouldn't say – let me think, maybe we should march to the left, or maybe to the right??? You would give a direct order. This is exactly what you are doing. This is not a request. You are in command at all times.

Always say thank you in some form. It can be simple, or it can be complicated, but it always has to be from the heart.

Remember these rules and how to deal with the Jinni beings, also look at the rules more in the beginning of my book and you will manifest a wonderful life.

We are meant to be happy. To have abundance and all our wishes fulfilled. We are here to learn and to do better. To learn to make better decisions, better choices and to evolve to a Higher Spiritual level within ourselves and have a better earthly life.

The Occult Rule is – Do No Harm!

JINNI CHARMS

There are Sigils-Signs-Seals for the Jinni that act much as a magnet to attract the vibration of the Jinni and to contain the intent and ability connected to a particular Jinn.

Copy the following Seals and carry them with you at all times to create the particular situation you wish to attract into your life.

Jinn named Saris

Intent: teaches how to make talisman and to ban unwanted beings.

Trace the Seal in blue or make a copy of it and trace over it in blue.

Jinn named Asoreg

Intent: connected to art via pictures. Painting, engraving, sewing, among other numerous forms.

Trace the Seal in blue or make a copy of it and trace over it in blue.

Jinn named Soteri

Intent: music. Inspirational to composers, connected to all forms of instruments, old and modern.

Trace the Seal in green or make a copy of it and trace over it in green.

Jinn named Mikael

Intent: master over your enemies. Helps politicians.

Trace the Seal in red or make a copy of it and trace over it in red.

Jinn named Jenuri
Intent: protection against negativity.

Trace the Seal in black or make a copy of it and trace over it in black.

Jinn named Zagriona

Intent: helps teaching on all levels. Writers, teachers, editors and so forth.

Trace the Seal in brown or make a copy of it and trace over it in brown.

DIVINE MAGICK

The Jinn named Milon aids you in understanding and connecting to Divine Magick, as well as being able to work with the Akashi records.

This knowledge helps the practitioner to work on all the planes of existence and have influence over them.

This Jinn also connects to the Law of Karma. The practitioner will be able to not only understand the concept, but be able to work with Karma to develop himself or herself.

Karmic Law states that whatever you do comes back to you. Good or bad. So we are much more aware of how we live, what we do, say or think. We never do anything negative (as much as realistically possible). We do not fear the afterlife. We've already been in contact with that realm. We are working on our Karma instead to gain enlightenment and progress on our personal evolution.

As always, do your self-defense first.

Focus your intent on one of the Jinns abilities at a time. Pick which one you wish to work with.

Find a quiet spot, preferably outside.

Relax your muscles with slow breathing.

Count slowly backward 3 to 1. Repeat this 3 times(3,3,3, 2,2,2, 1,1,1). Do this long enough to feel you are in your psychic, alpha state of mind.

Summoning the Millon:

I command and conjure Milon, the powerful Jinn to come to me at my bidding swiftly, peacefully and in a way as to harm none, NOW.

100% POSITIVE SPELLS AND INCANTATIONS FOR ALADDIN'S MAGICK LAMP

Open the book of knowledge to give me the insight that I now seek to be able to work with (specify which ability).

Help me to control the ability I wish to gain harming none, in a positive manner.

Thank you and go swiftly to do my command.

Go in harmony and love.

(Look upward toward the sky, stretching your arms above your head also toward the sky and say:)

As I say, so shall it be.

Stand for a minute or two and be aware of how you feel an any ideas that pop into our head.

Walk away, always paying attention to any insights or ideas that are sent from Milon.

BE A MODERN DAY PROPHET

Prophets have always been with us. Some call them psychics or intuitives. It all deals with prediction. It is all the same.

It means you are able to know things without utilizing your 5 senses.

We have all had these experiences, but perhaps weren't aware that it had a name for the ability.

Have you ever walked down a street and felt uncomfortable, as though there was someone following you? And when you turned around, there was. Now, that doesn't necessarily mean the person is dangerous to you. However, it is a survival instinct. If you are walking on the streets of Manhattan, there are always people walking behind you. How can there not be? The difference is that when the same person is doing so for a longer period of time, your guard goes up and your survival instinct kicks in. Again, you have to look at the situation. In a very crowded place, it usually doesn't have that meaning.

You can work with a Jinn to heighten these abilities inherent within you. If you so choose.

This Jinn is known as Eneki and is connected to the astrological sign of Gemini.

Wearing something brown in color will add to your control and connection to Eneki.

When you call on this Jinn, remember to do so with reverence and command. Be aware that when you enter into the realm of intuition, you don't always receive the information you would prefer.

You may find that someone who is cranky and seems negative is really a good person and just has defenses up. Or someone who seems your friend and positive is really negative.

We call on intuition in forms that are appropriate for us at this time. You may develop a higher sense of "knowing" or clairaudience, clairvoyance, dowsing or psychometry. You never know which way an ability will come to you. One technique is not better then another, as people have assumed. The point isn't how you receive the information. The point is to get the information correctly.

We always do psychic self-defense when we tune into prophetic information. This is so that we don't accidentally tune into any negative entities. If they are negative, they will lie. In which case, your information will not be correct and you may not be aware of it at the time.

The conjuring in a commanding voice:

Oh great and mighty Eneki, I conjure thee thus:

Come to me by the powers of the Divine.

Come to me in a peaceful, harmonious manner, harming none.

Bring to me the abilities of High intuition in ways that are appropriate forms for me at this time. Bring them swiftly in a way that I shall be aware of them and the knowledge of how to use them in a positive manner.

Eneki, bend to my will and obey my commands.

Thank you and go forth until I summon again.

And so it is.

After the conjuring, take a little time to allow yourself to pay attention to any intuitive urges or gaining an idea all of a sudden or any other feelings. Pay attention for the next few weeks so you become more familiar with these energies.

WATER ELEMENTALS

The element of water has been utilized for centuries in various forms.

It is considered a cleanser of negativity, a conductor of healing energy, a form for tuning into psychic abilities as a focal point, a connection to our physical bodies as water makes up so much of it, among other utilizations.

Water in the occult systems is also known to represent emotions.

A triangle with the point facing down represents the water element and the female principle.

When doing a conjuring, the triangle is where the Jinn or other spirit will appear and be held. The summoning is usually done from a circle of protection.

When we work with the elemental spirit of Jinn, we are also connecting to all forms of water. The oceans, streams, waterfalls and so on.

This in nature also connects us to any forms living in these waters. Minerals, vegetation, sea creatures- both in the physical realm and in the spiritual, mythical realms.

Before you call in the elemental spirit of the water, first and foremost pick which area you wish to work with. Is it for emotional reasons or connecting to a creature of the deep or (?).

Then decide what your intent is very specifically and in a concise manner. You have to have all of this done prior doing the summoning.

Once all this is done, wash your hands.

Put up your protection.

Get a goblet or glass of water to hold in your hand during the summoning.

<u>Summon the elemental Jinn Andrachor:</u>

I, <u>(say your name with pride and power)</u>, summon you, elemental Jinn Andrachor of all waters. You are proud to be connected to the astrological sign of Leo.

Come in a peaceful manner, in a physically pleasing manner and causing no harm to me or others.

I command thee to give me the insight and abilities needed so I can commune with the element of water. I am imbued by your element to manifest into my life (<u>state as a fact what your intent is at this time</u>).

Bring this, my desire, to me rapidly and so that I may be aware of it consciously.

As I summon you, come each time I call, swiftly and carry out my commands to the best of your abilities.

Go in peace, harmony and do my bidding now.

Thank you Andrachor. Go forth.

Take the goblet or glass of water that you've been holding and place it in your bedroom for 7 nights. Then take it, wash your hands in it and empty the rest of it anywhere outside your home.

THE LAW IS ON YOUR SIDE

The Laws made by man aren't necessarily the correct ones, nor are they always matching Spiritual Laws.

We call in the Jinn named Mimosah for all legal matters that are unjust, for human rights and for dealing with anyone (Ex: judges) connected with the law in any form.

Spiritual Laws are the ones we live by. However, we are still living in a society that has its own laws. Just or unjust.

This is the basic difference between the two as an example:

There are two tribes. The first tribe is attacking the second tribe and killing everyone. At the same time, the second tribe, in defense, is killing many of the first tribe.

Now, manmade law says both tribes are guilty and negative, because both are killing people.

Whereas, Spiritual Law says the first tribe is guilty because they are attacking and killing. But the second tribe is not guilty. The reason is that they are only killing for survival, not by choice. They are saving their families, themselves and everyone they can in the tribe.

So you can see the difference.

Calling in the Jinn Mimosah, is meant for the legal system in our society, but with cosmic laws to help us with justice.

Conjure this Jinn with a serious attitude when in need:

I conjure and command you, Mimosah, to appear before me this very instant. Come to me in peace, harming none.

Be ready to aid me in my situation (state what the situation is concisely and with details) when next I call.

61

Be ready to aid me in this endeavor so that the outcome is in my favor.

Do this hurting none.

Put into motion now what needs to be done for (name your situation) to be to my benefit.

Thank you and go forth to form the future and come quickly when next I call.

Go !

When you next deal with anyone connected to the legal system, lawyer, judge, jury or anyone else, make sure you wear something pink if possible. It can be any shade. Some men's shirts are such a light shade, they look almost white. Make sure the color is visible. You want people to see the color on you. This will also put them more in your favor, even if you don't say anything.

While dealing with these people, call mentally the name of the Jinn to come and help you during this process. Tell Mimosah thank you and to leave when that situation is over, until you call again.

LUCKY TRAVELS

The Jinn Egention, will make sure you are safe and your plans during travel don't go awry.

Carry the Seal of Egention during any form of travel.

Copy the Seal or make a copy and trace over it in the color blue.

During the summoning, hold the Seal of Egention in your hand.

Do the summoning:

I call forth Egention, to do my bidding. I command you to come to me in a peaceful, calm manner, harming none.

Through wind and hail, through fire and earth, throughout the times I will be traveling, keep me safe. Have all my plans go as expected and better. Make it so I have happy travel experiences.

Stay with me and keep me safe from beginning to the end of my wanderings.

Come when I call, I now Command.

Thank you and go forth to your realm until I call.

And as I say, so shall it be.

It is now completed. Take the Seal and place it in a secure place where others will not touch it.

Anytime you travel, carry this Seal with you. It is now activated.

WISHES MANIFEST

To manifest your desires and wishes, tell the atomic and molecular Divine Intelligence elements inherent within water, fire, air, earth and spirit.

We / you are able to impregnate anything with your desires and clear intentions.

Put up your self-defense protection.

Wash your hands under running water, letting all negativity around and permeating within you to run down.

Get seriously focused on your intent.

With white chalk, draw a triangle on the ground. Or use a staff or sword to draw in the earth. Start drawing your triangle from the left bottom point, then to the tip at the top and back down to the bottom right, next go left until it connects to the starting line. This is to contain the elemental nature spirit, known as the Jinn.

With white chalk, draw your magick circle. Start drawing toward the right, around you, until you completed the circle back to the beginning line.

Stand in the center of the circle, as always.

The conjuring:

I conjure thus: I now command the Great Jinn connected to all of the elements. To air, earth, fire, water and to spirit. I call on you to come swiftly and peacefully, harming none.

Know that I, (say our name), have power over you and command you to manifest my desire (state your purpose now).

By the power of 7 times 3, I command you to do my bidding. I am the Master who creates through you, the magnificent intents to bring into this physical realm.

64

My desire is focused, clear and positive. We harm none in gaining my goal.

I, (say your name), am Master over all I desire through my will and knowledge given by Divine Intelligence.

Come promptly and with good intentions when I summon you.

Thank you and go forth to put into motion creating the future to manifest into the physical plane my intent now.

Go forth until I call again and then come to me from wherever you are with rapid speed, in a positive way.

At this time, spend a minute in thankful prayer or thought.

Open the circle by smudging the chalk line, in reverse order, toward the left.

Step out and open the triangle in reverse order.

Walk away and don't look back.

Each morning, take 7 inhalations and with each and every one, focus on your intent.

Each and every night, repeat the morning ritual.

Do this to key everything from waking to evening.

CALL TO NATURE'S ABUNDANCE

With the help of the Jinn, you are about to open a door to unlimited abundance.

We are meant to be happy and to have the control, as mankind, over spirits who want to help us. That is their job. We are simply letting them do so, with our intent and commands. We also thank them, so we are in essence, paying them with positive energies.

We don't force the door to open. That doesn't work. Nature can have a stubborn streak...

1 - Get comfortable and relax.

2 - With white chalk, draw a triangle on the ground. Or use a staff or sword to draw in the earth. Start drawing your triangle from the left bottom point, then to the tip at the top and back down to the bottom right, next go left until it connects to the starting line. This is to contain the elemental nature spirit, known as the Jinn.

3 - With white chalk, draw your magick circle. Start drawing toward the right, around you, until you completed the circle back to the beginning line.

4 - Stand in the center of your circle.

5 - After you "shield up", you can <u>conjure:</u>

I, the Master of my destiny, (<u>say your name</u>), call forth the Jinn of the Open Door , to create unlimited abundance into my life.

Come now in haste and peacefully, harming none.

I now, safely and always protected, place my awareness in front of my heart. I open my heart to the Oneness with nature.

I am One with nature, the universe and all of creation through your help. Therefore, all things come to me easily, freely without hindrance or delay. I love nature (birds, animals and so on) in all forms and they love me. I can communicate with them easily and they do with me.

As a co-creator of the Divine, and with the help of the Master Jinn of Nature, I call upon and magnetize my energy so that all good things will flow to me easily at will. Therefore, as I inhale all good things come freely and easily to me whenever I decree and deem it to be. Manifesting, materializing. As I exhale my Dinvine magickal intent, it is sent into the ethers where it will manifest and multiply with the help of the Master Jinn of Nature.

6 - At this time, spend a minute in giving thanks.

7 - Open the circle by smudging the chalk line, or the line in the earth, in reverse order, toward the left.

8 - Step out and open the triangle in reverse order.

BLESSINGS OF THE JINN

Blessings are considered God's favor and His protection.

Blessings come in many forms. They can come from our Source through a shaman, a spiritual leader and others or from the spirit plane to help to improve our lives.

The Jinn are an ancient and powerful race. As mentioned previously, they were here before Adam. To gain a Jinni blessing is a powerful blessing indeed.

1 - Do your protection.

2 - Cleanse your body, mind and spirit of all negativity.

3 - Approach this Jinn with reverence.

4 - Now comes the conjuring:

I, (say your name with a commanding voice), bid you, the Jinn of Blessings, to Bless me in all of my undertakings hence forward.

I call on you to Bless me in the name of the Most High, the Source of us all.

I shall, to the bests of my abilities, only do positive. In keeping with honoring your Blessing, given to me upon this day.

(Stand for a little while, for as long as you are comfortable, breathing slowly and focusing on accepting the Blessing.)

Thank you Jinn of Blessings and come to me whenever I call, swiftly, from wherever you may be.

Go back from whence you came.

5 - Spend the rest of the day being aware that you are blessed and go about your business in joy and harmony.

BANISH NEGATIVITY

This Jinn helps you to banish all negativity from your life. At times, we are overwhelmed by all that is surrounding us and by the negative energies from those around us. Even positive friends may turn negative through time. Just as negative people can become more positive.

We call upon the Jinn of Banishing

Get focused on your intent of getting rid of negativity around you, in a positive way.

With white chalk, draw a triangle on the ground. Start drawing your triangle from the left bottom point, then to the tip at the top and back down to the bottom right, next go left until it connects to the starting line. Containing the elemental spirit, known as the Jinn.

With white chalk, draw your magick circle. Start drawing toward the right, around you, until you completed the circle back to the beginning line.

Stand in the center of the Magick Circle.

Do the magickal invocation:

I now envoke the power of the Jinn of Banishing.

I call forth this Jinn to do my bidding. To banish the negativity surrounding me, which now limits and slows me down from my rightful place in life.

Banish, I command you, all negative friends and people from my life in a positive way. Harming none and elevating them to their Higher Good, away from me.

And as I also put out positive energy, the Occult Law states that like attracts like.

I now manifest positive, nice people around me.

Go forth and clear the way for me, that nothing stops or blocks me from my good, in a positive way.

Thank you and go in love and peace until I call on you.

Focus on a thankful prayer or make one up to the Jinn for helping you to overcome these negative energies.

At this time, give thanks.

Open the circle by smudging the chalk line, in reverse order, toward the left.

Step out and open the triangle in reverse order.

Go about your day.

DECODING RELIGION

The Jinn can help you to understand and decode all religious systems.

Do not misunderstand this. It has nothing to do with changing anything you have your faith in. It doesn't say that any particular religion is better than any other.

What you will learn is what various belief systems really believe in and what they actually represent.

As an example: You may read a book and say to yourself, this part is Truth and this part is the authors' opinion. Not good or bad. Simply you will be able to recognize the Spiritual Truth contained within the writing from opinion. Normally, we can't always tell, because it's the same person writing throughout the book.

Get relaxed. Take 3 deep, slow breaths, counting from 3 to 1, 3 times (3,3,3, 2,2,2, 1,1,1). This connects you to your alpha , psychic state of mind quicker.

Put your protection up.

Take a minute to focus your intent.

With white chalk, draw a triangle on the ground. Start drawing your triangle from the left bottom point, then to the tip at the top and back down to the bottom right, next go left until it connects to the starting line. Containing the elemental Jinn.

With white chalk, draw your magick circle. Start drawing toward the right, around you, until you completed the circle back to the beginning line.

Stand in the center of your circle.

Do your <u>conjuring:</u>

I now call in, in a peaceful, positive manner, the Jinn known as Eralicarison and harming no one.

I declare and order you to give me the knowledge and the intuitive insight to understand the true meaning of any religion I delve into. In Truth we learn, in Truth we live in a positive way.

Show me the ways that shall enhance my life. That I may live in the Spiritual Truth of my choosing, that fits me.

Do so now and do my bidding quickly, any time I summon you.

Thank you Eralicarison.

Go forth.

As I say, so shall it be.

Know that it is done.

Open the circle by smudging the chalk line, or the line in the earth, in reverse order, toward the left.

Step out and open the triangle in reverse order.

DEFEAT YOUR ENEMIES

Try as we might, no matter what we do, there are people who are just plain negative, vengeful, jealous, greedy, mean and just plain bad.

We cannot change these people. We understand that they don't know any better and they are not on a spiritually elevated level yet. That doesn't mean we are alright with it.

We are positive and try to always do right, but that doesn't mean that we are martyrs. We are not supposed to be passive and a doormat. We aren't here to be unhappy and to put up with intolerable situations.

Even in the Christian religion, at one point in the Bible, it says that Jesus threw the merchants off the temple stairs.

We have our limits. We try to do things in a positive way, but when it goes over the line, we need to step back, reassess and decide what we are willing to put up with. And why?

We call on the Jinn Veubiah for this purpose.

1 - Draw or copy the Seal of Veubiah. Do this in red.

2 - Do your protection (as I always say, Shield Up).

3 - Wash your hands.

4 -Hold the Seal throughout the summoning.

5 -Focus.

6 - With white chalk, draw a triangle on the ground. Start drawing your triangle from the left bottom point, then to the tip at the top and back down to the bottom right, next go left until it connects to the starting line.

7 - With white chalk, draw the circle. Start drawing toward the right, around you, until you completed the circle back

to the beginning line.

8 - Stand in the center of your circle.

<u>Conjure thus:</u>

I call forth the Powerful and Great Jinn, Veubiah. Come to me swiftly, peacefully, in a comely appearance, causing no harm to me or anyone else.

Come and be known to me in a positive manner, to aid me in defeating my enemies. To be Victorious ! To have all of my enemies banished from my life in a way that does no harm to them.

For even though my enemies do not wish me well, and some may wish me harm, I shall not falter from my positive Path. I shall not go down to their level. I shall stay in the Light.

Help me to discover the plans of my enemies, so they may be thwarted.

With you, Veubiah, I will overcome my foes.

Thank you Veubiah, and come swiftly when next I call upon you, no matter where you may be at the time.

Go forth and begin this very instant to carry out my commands, now.

And as I say, so shall it be.

9 -Open the circle by smudging the chalk line, in reverse order, toward the left.

10 - Step out and open the triangle in reverse order.

11 – Carry the Seal with you at all times.

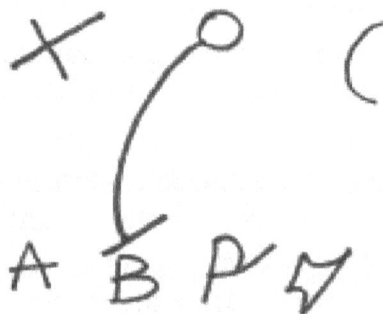

MONEY SUCCESS

Money comes through to you in various forms. This Jinn is connected to success and financial gain through your profession. Whether in an analytical job, as head of a company, as a homemaker, in the arts, with the trades or any other form of work, the Jinn Alagill, will help you to create the success you desire.

This Jinn creates not only the success in your occupation, but the financial success that goes with it. After all, we are in a physical body. We need to eat, get to work and do other mundane things.

I always look at it this way- the more you have, the better you can help others. After all, if your friend needs a ride to work because his car broke down, you need to be able to have a car (which takes money) to help drive him to work. Who are you going to be able to help if you are starving? You'll be too busy working on survival. So let's get moving on improving your life and the life of those around you.

Put up your protection.

Focus on your intent.

Know that you are creating success and money.

Summoning the Jinn Alagill:

I summon and command you, Jinn of finance and success, Alagill, to come to me NOW.

I command you to come in a positive way, harming none.

Come and heighten my abilities and my opportunities to make wealth. Create for me, situations that bring money and success in a positive way for all. That puts me in my Right profession, so that I may work competently, easily, happily and successfully with professional ethics.

Have others see that in truth, I am trustworthy, a person of my word, dependable and do the best job possible for everyone. Have them see all my positive abilities.

Help me to move up in finance and success.

Shape the future, such that all of this occurs rapidly, in a positive manner.

Come when I next summon you with great haste from wherever you may be at the time, in a peaceful, calm manner.

Thank you Alagill.

Go forth to create my command, now.

So it is.

Do your best each day, knowing you have the help of this Jinn and that your success is on the way already.

CONCLUSION

WE ARE THE SOLUTION.

Remember with unbridled Jinn, anything can happen. You have to maintain your attitude of control, knowing full well that we, in the physical body, have the free will and so the control over other realms.

You are the keeper of your soul and your destiny. The positive Jinn are there to help you, so call on them. They are readily available to you.

Make sure you do any work with them with sincerity. They can tell the difference. Without any trepidation. You are the master, the controlling force.

Protect yourself at all times, through any psychic self-defense form or prayer of protection.

These are proven powerful formulae.

Get your magickal self up and go forth into your better, happier life.

YES YOU CAN !!!

ADVERTISEMENT

80

www.ingramcontent.com/pod-product-compliance
Lightning Source LLC
Chambersburg PA
CBHW060137050426
42448CB00010B/2177